THE OFFICIAL
WEST BROMWICH ALBION
ANNUAL 2020

WRITTEN BY DAVE BOWLER
DESIGNED BY LUCY BOYD

A Grange Publication

© 2019. Published by Grange Communications Ltd., Edinburgh, under licence from West Bromwich Albion Football Club. Printed in the EU.

Every effort has been made to ensure the accuracy of information within this publication but the publishers cannot be held responsible for any errors or omissions. Views expressed are those of the author and do not necessarily represent those of the publishers or the football club. All rights reserved.

Photographs © West Bromwich Albion Football Club, Laurie Rampling and AMA Photography.

ISBN 978-1-913034-33-7

CONTENTS

WEST BILIĆ ALBION!

Albion were delighted to secure the services of Slaven Bilić as the Club's new Head Coach over the course of the summer.

The experienced 50-year-old former Premier League and international boss agreed a two-year contract and set to work immediately on the task of heading up Albion's Sky Bet Championship challenge for 2019/20.

Slaven takes up The Hawthorns post having led his nation, Croatia, to two European Championships and delivered a record-breaking Premier League performance for West Ham United, who achieved a highest-placed finish and goals scored during his two-year stay there.

In top-level European football, which has taken in spells at Hajduk Split, Lokomotiv Moscow and Besiktas, Slaven has built up an impressive 46 per cent win ratio and he now turns his attention to leading a new promotion challenge with the Baggies.

He said, "I'm delighted with this opportunity of course. We want to improve, we want to improve on the pitch and Albion have convinced me they want to return to the Premier League. Albion have a short-term project and a long-term project and they do not clash.

" I am really proud. It's a big responsibility but I am really excited.

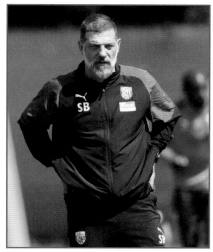

> **" I'm not English, but I have spent lots of my life playing or managing here and it was my wish to come back.**

"They wanted me to lead them, to help improve them. They made it clear they wanted me to be the one to lead them in this and I didn't think twice once they had spoken to me.

"It's a massive club because of the history and the fans. They are very demanding but they are very loyal. It's a traditional club and it's a family club, but also very, very big. We are going to try to come back to the Premier League this year. Short-term or long-term, this is where this club belongs.

"When I heard about the project and the ambition, it made me very tempted for this job and from there I only had positive thoughts. It only took me one day to say 'yes'. It wasn't a big negotiation. I wanted to come here. The club really wanted me and they showed that, which is the most important thing. I am really proud. It's a big responsibility but I am really excited.

"It's not easy to play here for opposition teams, you know. I remember even the game where West Ham won 3-0. The first 15 minutes it was like we were under so much pressure. You could feel the crowd, you feel the noise, you feel the pressure. And that is also one of the reasons why I came here. It is one of these clubs and grounds where you can really still use that kind of atmosphere to help you. To be like a hostile, home crowd.

"And to be fair, when I didn't know that I was coming here, I watched both the Play-Off games against Villa. That atmosphere in the second game, you could feel it back home where I was watching it. You could feel it on the TV. It was bouncing, it was buzzing, and then I spoke about that game in a coffee shop afterwards and my friends were telling me the same – that it was proper football.

"The Championship was always on my bucket list. It's one of my boxes that I wanted to tick off and now I have the opportunity to be the manager of a massive club in this league.

"I would like to thank West Bromwich Albion for the opportunity to manage such a big club. It's a privilege. I'm not English, but I have spent lots of my life playing or managing here and it was my wish to come back.

"The Hawthorns is a beautiful stadium. Perfect. The training ground is a football training ground. In the modern age, players are already dragged away from the essence of football. It's all perfect for them, but you want the smell of grass. And ours is exactly that. It's got everything. It's new, the canteen is brilliant but it's not a luxury hotel. It shouldn't be and I like it. This is football."

SEASON REVIEW
AUGUST

Albion's return to the Championship gave us a pretty quick reminder of just how busy life can get at the lower level with five league games – and a couple of League Cup ties – crammed into just 24 days!

Things didn't get off to the right start unfortunately, a packed Hawthorns on opening day watching in disbelief as we were beaten 2-1 by Bolton Wanderers, though a goal from Harvey Barnes suggested we were going to enjoy watching a special talent in the months ahead.

Another one of those arrived before our midweek trip to Nottingham Forest, Dwight Gayle joining the party on loan from Newcastle United. Dwight was a late sub for the Throstles as we salvaged a draw late on through a thumping finish from Matt Phillips.

The following weekend, we got our first three points of the campaign in a crazy 4-3 game at Norwich City, Jay Rodriguez scoring twice, then it was the turn of the Albion youngsters to help see us past Luton in the League Cup; Oli Burke getting the game's only goal.

We properly kicked into gear in our next game, going berserk against QPR, scoring seven goals to their one, Rodriguez and

Phillips with a brace apiece as Rangers simply couldn't get anywhere near us especially in a second half mauling.

Unfortunately, we'd used up all our goals for when we made the long Friday night trip to Middlesbrough we lost 1-0 to a late Boro goal, much to Tony Pulis' delight. It was back on track the following Tuesday though, Jonathan Leko and Kyle Edwards grabbing their first goals for the Throstles as we defeated Mansfield 2-0 in the League Cup to see out the first month of the season.

SEPTEMBER

We couldn't have started the month in brighter fashion, beating Stoke 2-1 at The Hawthorns, two fine goals coming from Gayle, including the one that would prove to be our goal of the season.

We returned from the international break to tough out a 1-1 draw at Birmingham, Sam Johnstone saving a penalty, then a crazy game at home under the lights against Bristol City ended with Albion 4-2 winners, the ball going from end to end as both sides went hell for leather for the win.

Following that, we produced a much more controlled 90 minutes to send Millwall packing

2-0, the result never in doubt, but an Andros Townsend masterclass was enough to send us packing from the League Cup, beaten 3-0 at The Hawthorns by Premier League Crystal Palace.

We recovered well though, rounding off the month with a trip to Deepdale to take on Preston North End, coming home with three points and a 3-2 win, Rodriguez and Gayle continuing their battle at the top of the scoring charts with another goal each.

SEASON REVIEW

OCTOBER

It was the Harvey Barnes show at Hillsborough, Albion toiling at 2-0 down into the last ten minutes only for the Leicester loanee to force an own goal from a Sheffield Wednesday man, then go on a mazy 50-yard run before sticking the ball into the Owls' net to grab us what had looked an unlikely draw.

We struggled early on against Reading at home that Saturday, but another steamroller of a second half was enough to see us through to an emphatic 4-1 win to go into the next international break. We were slow coming out of it though, losing 1-0 at Wigan, then we got caught cold in midweek, Derby scoring early and often as they beat us 4-1 at The Hawthorns.

Blackburn somehow escaped with a 1-1 draw on the Saturday, despite being down to ten men and with a defender in goal, but we ended the month in fifth place in the table and still well in the hunt for promotion.

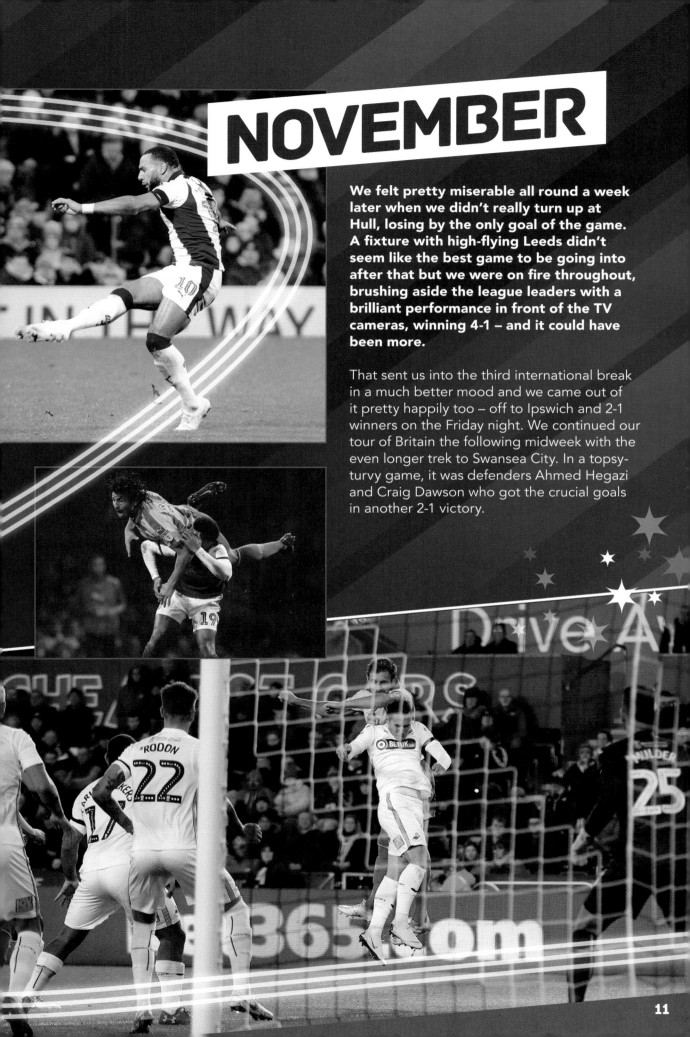

NOVEMBER

We felt pretty miserable all round a week later when we didn't really turn up at Hull, losing by the only goal of the game. A fixture with high-flying Leeds didn't seem like the best game to be going into after that but we were on fire throughout, brushing aside the league leaders with a brilliant performance in front of the TV cameras, winning 4-1 – and it could have been more.

That sent us into the third international break in a much better mood and we came out of it pretty happily too – off to Ipswich and 2-1 winners on the Friday night. We continued our tour of Britain the following midweek with the even longer trek to Swansea City. In a topsy-turvy game, it was defenders Ahmed Hegazi and Craig Dawson who got the crucial goals in another 2-1 victory.

DECEMBER

Six games faced us in a busy December and we seemed to be off to a great start with some Monday night football against Brentford, on top and in control, but just a goal ahead. Guess what happened right at the end? Yes, they equalised...

It was our turn to dig out a late draw on the Friday night though, twice behind against Aston Villa before the hand of Rod helped us to square things up at 2-2 in the final seconds. It was back to winning ways the following Friday, standing up to an early battering at Sheffield United before a Gareth Barry masterclass turned the tide and saw us to a 2-1 win.

Yorkshire was good to us because, just over a week later, we were back again, this time at Rotherham's New York Stadium, battering them 4-0, Gayle helping himself to a hat-trick, the Millers even missing a penalty to the embarrassment of the stadium DJ who had started playing the goal music as the kick was taken!

Boxing Day gave us the chance to get some revenge over Wigan and we did, winning 2-0, and then our final game of 2018 went all the way to the wire, Chris Brunt's last-gasp goal getting us a 1-1 draw with his old club Sheffield Wednesday, Albion ending the year in third place in the table, nicely positioned for a new year attack on promotion.

JANUARY

The new year got off to an unhappy start though, Jake Livermore sent off as we lost 2-1 at Blackburn Rovers, but we put things right in the FA Cup with another win over Wigan, just ten days after we'd beaten them in the Championship.

Surprise table toppers Norwich were next up at The Hawthorns and despite Gayle's goal after just 12 minutes, a tight game ended 1-1 with the Canaries doing what they managed to do all season, score a game-changing late goal.

We had a Monday night in Bolton next as their fans protested at the way the club was being run, supporters hurling tennis balls on the pitch at the start of the televised game. It didn't upset our concentration at all and we eased to a 2-0 win with goals from Rodriguez and Sam Field. Field played his part on the Saturday too as a youthful Albion ground out a 0-0 draw at Brighton in the FA Cup.

FEBRUARY

February was full of very tough-looking fixtures, none harder than a visit from Tony Pulis' Middlesbrough right at the start. They took an early lead, Gayle and Rodriguez – who else? – put us in front, before an inspired substitution brought Assombalonga onto the pitch to grab two late Boro goals and turn the game on its head.

We took Brighton all the way to extra-time before bowing out of the FA Cup in midweek, but we were back on track soon enough with a 1-0 win in a pretty dull game at Stoke – aren't they all!

A frantic game with Nottingham Forest ended 2-2 as Claudio Yacob made his return to The Hawthorns with the visitors, then we were always in control at Villa Park the following Saturday as we won 2-0, Hal Robson-Kanu and Rodriguez doing the damage to the Villans. When we then won a dramatic game at QPR, Livermore scoring in the final seconds to clinch a 3-2 victory, things seemed to be going our way on the road to promotion.

But never count your chickens before they're hatched. A scrappy game against Sheffield United followed at The Hawthorns and the 1-0 win that they eked out was a damaging blow to our chances.

MARCH

The bad news kept coming the following Friday as we travelled to Elland Road and the kind of atmosphere we hadn't seen for a while. Leeds started like a whirlwind and throughout the game we struggled to handle them, eventually tumbling to a 4-0 defeat as they avenged their Hawthorns humiliation from earlier in the season.

When we were then held 1-1 at home by bottom of the table Ipswich eight days later, the Albion board decided to part company with Head Coach Darren Moore, first team coach Jimmy Shan taking over from him for the rest of the season.

The rest of the month could hardy have gone better. Swansea were brushed aside 3-0, including a comical penalty miss from the Swans when Celina managed to move the ball about 30cm forward as he slipped while taking the kick!

It was the Kyle Edwards show at Brentford as the youngster produced a mesmerising run into the penalty area and past several defenders before scoring the only goal of the game and we ended March by coming from behind twice to beat Birmingham at home, Livermore smashing in the crucial late winner from the edge of the box.

APRIL

Automatic promotion hopes were still realistic going into April, but the first two games of the month pretty much finished them off. A 2-0 defeat at Millwall was followed by a 20-minute collapse at Bristol City and even though we fought back to make it 3-2, defeat there left us with just too much to do – it was going to have to be the play-offs.

We started to get ourselves into good condition by going through the rest of April unbeaten. We wiped the floor with Preston, winning 4-1 at The Hawthorns, Gayle claiming a second hat-trick of the season, then we saw off Hull City 3-2 in an entertaining Hawthorns tussle on Good Friday.

We completed the Easter programme with a 0-0 draw at Reading and then played the final home game of the normal season, coming from behind once more to beat Rotherham United 2-1, sending them down to League One in the process.

MAY

The 46-game season ended in a 3-1 defeat at Derby County, results there and elsewhere meaning that our play-off opponents would be Aston Villa, the first leg at Villa Park, but without Robson-Kanu, who was sent off late in the game at Derby.

Things all started so well at the Villa, Gayle giving us an early first half lead, after which we defended strongly until Gayle was booked for time wasting just past the hour. That seemed to knock us off balance and Villa grabbed their opportunity, turning the tie around with two goals in four minutes from Hourihane and Abraham. Worse was to follow, Gayle booked a second time in the 88th minute, thereby ending his season in suspension.

There was still all to play for in the second leg at The Hawthorns though and a Dawson header in the 29th minute squared things up. In a fabulous, frantic Hawthorns atmosphere, Albion battered

Villa early on in the second half but couldn't find that breakthrough and gradually the visitors started to threaten again.

When Brunt was sent off 10 minutes from time, it looked all up, but a huge effort from the Throstles saw us through into extra-time and then all the way through to penalties. Sadly, it was not to be and the Villa won the shootout 4-3 to book their passage to Wembley and leave us wondering just what might have been…

SEASON RESULTS

Date	Opponent	Score	Scorers
Saturday 4 August	Bolton Wanderers	1-2	Barnes
Tuesday 7 August	Nottingham Forest (ko 7.45pm)	1-1	Phillips
Saturday 11 August	Norwich City	4-3	Rodriguez 2, Barnes, Robson-Kanu
Tuesday 14 August	Luton Town (Lc1) (ko 8pm)	1-0	Burke
Saturday 18 August	Queens Park Rangers	7-1	Phillips 2, Rodriguez 2, Robson-Kanu, Gayle, Gibbs
Friday 24 August	Middlesbrough (ko 7.45pm)	0-1	
Tuesday 28 August	Mansfield Town (Lc2) (ko 8pm)	2-1	Leko, Edwards
Saturday 1 September	Stoke City	2-1	Gayle 2
Friday 14 September	Birmingham City (ko 7.45pm)	1-1	Phillips
Tuesday 18 September	Bristol City (ko 8pm)	4-2	Rodriguez 2 , Barnes, Gayle
Saturday 22 September	Millwall	2-0	Gibbs, own goal
Tuesday 25 September	Crystal Palace (Lc3) (ko 8pm)	0-3	
Saturday 29 September	Preston North End	3-2	Gayle, Rodriguez, own goal
Wednesday 3 October	Sheffield Wednesday (ko 7.45pm)	2-2	Barnes, own goal
Saturday 6 October	Reading	4-1	Gayle 2, Barnes, Bartley
Saturday 20 October	Wigan Athletic	0-1	
Wednesday 24 October	Derby County (ko 8pm)	1-4	Rodriguez
Saturday 27 October	Blackburn Rovers	1-1	Dawson
Saturday 3 November	Hull City	0-1	
Saturday 10 November	Leeds United (ko 5.30pm)	4-1	Phillips, Barnes, Robson-Kanu, Gayle
Friday 23 November	Ipswich Town (ko 7.45pm)	2-1	Rodriguez, Barnes
Wednesday 28 November	Swansea City (ko 7.45pm)	2-1	Hegazi, Dawson
Monday 3 December	Brentford (ko 8pm)	1-1	Barnes, own goal
Friday 7 December	Aston Villa (ko 8pm)	2-2	Gayle, Rodriguez
Friday 14 December	Sheffield United (ko 7.45pm)	2-1	Barry, Gibbs
Saturday 22 December	Rotherham United	4-0	Barnes, Gayle 3

2018/19

WEST BROMWICH ALBION

Saturday 29 December	Sheffield Wednesday	1-1	Brunt
Tuesday 1 January	Blackburn Rovers	1-2	Rodriguez
Saturday 5 January	Wigan Athletic (FA Cup 3) (ko 12.30pm)	1-0	Sako
Saturday 12 January	Norwich City	1-1	Gayle
Monday 21 January	Bolton Wanderers (ko 8pm)	2-0	Rodriguez, Field
Saturday 26 January	Brighton (FA Cup 4)	0-0	
Saturday 2 February	Middlesbrough	2-3	Rodriguez, Gayle
Wednesday 6 February	Brighton (FA Cup 4R) (ko 8.05pm)	1-3	Bartley
Saturday 9 February	Stoke City (ko 5.30pm)	1-0	Gayle
Tuesday 12 February	Nottingham Forest (ko 8pm)	2-2	Murphy, Rodriguez
Saturday 16 February	Aston Villa	2-0	Rodriguez, Robson-Kanu
Tuesday 19 February	Queens Park Rangers (ko 7.45pm)	3-2	Montero, Murphy, Livermore
Saturday 23 February	Sheffield United (ko 5.30pm)	0-1	
Friday 1 March	Leeds United (ko 7.45pm)	0-4	
Saturday 9 March	Ipswich Town	1-1	Johansen
Wednesday 13 March	Swansea City (ko 8pm)	3-0	Brunt, Holgate, Rodriguez
Saturday 16 March	Brentford	1-0	Edwards
Friday 29 March	Birmingham City (ko 8pm)	3-2	Gayle, Rodriguez, Livermore
Saturday 6 April	Millwall	0-2	
Tuesday 9 April	Bristol City (ko 7.45pm)	2-3	Rodriguez, Gayle
Saturday 13 April	Preston North End	4-1	Rodriguez, Gayle 3
Friday 19 April	Hull City	3-2	Gayle 2, Gibbs
Monday 22 April	Reading	0-0	
Saturday 27 April	Rotherham United	2-1	Rodriguez, Harper
Sunday 5 May	Derby County (ko 12.30pm)	1-3	Johansen
Saturday 11 May	Aston Villa (Po Sf 1) (ko 12.30pm)	1-2	Gayle
Tuesday 14 May	Aston Villa (Po Sf 2) (ko 8pm)	1-0	Dawson (Aston Villa won 4-3 on penalties)

GOAL OF THE SEASON!

Dwight Gayle was the man who persuaded the fans to vote for him in the Goal of the Season Awards for 2018/19. His memorable first goal against Stoke City in the 2-1 home victory in September was the pick of some terrific Albion goals across the campaign.

The goal was a thing of beauty as we played our way through Stoke from back to front, beginning with Sam Johnstone's roll out from his area. Ultimately, Kieran Gibbs saw the chance to drive towards the Stoke box before feeding the ball to Gayle under a challenge from McClean.

One sublime, twinkle-toed 180 degree turn later and Gayle had left the Stoke defence behind, only to see Butland hurtling towards him. Allowing the keeper to commit himself, Gayle skipped around him and slipped the ball into the waiting goal, a lovely finish – and a goal of the season!

A FILIP TO ALBION'S PROMOTION CHANCES!

Albion's first summer signing ahead of 2019/20 was Croatian midfielder Filip Krovinović, who joined the Throstles on a season-long loan from Benfica.

The 23-year-old earned caps with Croatia U19s and U21s, winning promotion in his home country with NK Zagreb before joining Rio Ave in Portugal four years ago. He now has 19 first team appearances to his name at Benfica after joining the Portuguese giants in 2017.

He started out with Lokomotiva Zagreb and Dinamo Zagreb at youth level before joining NK Zagreb, where he made his senior debut in 2013.

Krovinović played a prominent role in NK Zagreb's Second Division title-winning campaign in 2013/14. He then went on to establish himself as one of the best players in the Croatian top flight the following season, helping his side secure a fifth-placed finish in their first season back in the MAXtv Prva Liga.

A move away followed in August 2015 as he joined up with Portuguese Primeira Liga team Rio Ave. After an initial campaign settling in to new surroundings, Krovinović began to really catch the eye in his second season and netted five times in 33 games as his side finished seventh in the league.

Filip's performances for Rio Ave attracted attention from Portugal's most successful club, Benfica. The midfielder joined in June 2017, signing a five-year contract.

During his first two seasons at the Estádio da Luz, Krovinović featured for Benfica in the UEFA Europa League and also helped the club to the 2018/19 Primeira Liga title.

Filip said, "This is my first time in England and it will be a new challenge. I hope that I will conquer the challenge and play lots of games here.

"The coach, Slaven Bilić, knows me, and I know his work. He was coach of the national team and he did a great job there, as well as at West Ham and Besiktas. I am very proud to come here and play for the club and for Slaven Bilić.

"The Croatian coaching staff will make it easier for me to settle because we speak the same language. Slaven can teach me a lot of things because he is a great manager."

Krovinović arrives at The Hawthorns with a reputation of being technically gifted.

"I am a number eight or a number 10. I'm a technical player. I like to have the ball and I like to control the game. Of course, everybody likes to score and assist also.

"I haven't set myself any goals or targets I'm just focused on playing well for West Bromwich Albion."

YOUNG PLAYER
OF THE SEASON

Rekeem Harper rounded off his breakthrough season in resounding fashion when he was awarded Albion's Young Player of the Year trophy.

He collected the gong from the legendary Tony Brown before the final home league game of the season against Rotherham United, and went on to celebrate in grand manner by scoring his first Albion goal in the 2-1 win – Bomber must have been giving him lessons!

Rekeem Harper

The accomplished midfielder made 19 starts and another four appearances off the bench for the Throstles during the 2018/109 season as he began to establish himself at the heart of the Albion side.

But after making that impact, the hard work starts now – it's the player of the year award that's next in his sights!

MORE SUCCESS FOR WBA BLIND TEAM!

WBA Blind retained their National League Cup at the end of 2018/19 with a dramatic penalty shootout victory against the Royal National College for the Blind.

Winners of the Brian Aaron's Cup in 2018, this 2019 win was even more memorable for the team after playing their final two games a man down due to an untimely injury.

Along the way, the side defeated current league champions Merseyside Blind, a team that boasts four England international players. Couple all that with stormy conditions and it's no wonder that The Albion Foundation Head of Disability and WBA Blind Head Coach, Paul Glover, was proud of his team's achievement.

"The side fought against adversity. For all the players and all the teams, the conditions were terrible for blind football," said Paul. "It became quite dangerous, but for the players to battle through in the manner that they did and to retain the trophy was exceptional."

Assisted by coach and guide Rich Henderson, Paul was pleased with the mentality of his side.

"The grit and the determination of the lads to keep battling against the odds, when on paper we shouldn't have had the success that we had, has allowed us to come through and be successful in the end," he said.

England international Darren Harris notched a hat-trick in the final against RNC for Albion but, given the tough circumstances, was as surprised as the rest of his team that they succeeded for a second season.

"We were all in shock really that we won it," said Darren. "I don't think we went into the tournament thinking that we had much of a chance. Things just came together, it was a real team effort.

"The weather was appalling, it was windy, it was wet, it was cold and we had a really tough schedule of fixtures as well. Football is a crazy game sometimes and someone was looking down on us I think!"

Added to his trio of goals, Darren also slotted home the decisive penalty in the shootout, ensuring the trophy was once again coming back to the West Midlands.

"I think it's the biggest victory that we've had," he said. "None of our team are young but I think when you've got something to play for, somehow you get a little bit more out of your body I guess – I'm sure they will be really sore afterwards!"

WHEN THE BALL HITS THE GOAL...
IT'S ZOHORE...

Albion found themselves a number nine in the summer with the signing of Danish striker Kenneth Zohore.

Having won promotion from the Championship with former club Cardiff City, Zohore knows all about the job in hand. The 6ft 2in striker has 23 Championship goals to his name, with two and a half seasons worth of playing experience at that level, before clocking up 20 Premier League appearances last term.

Kenneth made his debut at the age of 16 years and 35 days old, becoming the youngest player ever to do so in the Danish Superliga. Still aged 16, Zohore played for Copenhagen against Barcelona at the Nou Camp and became one of the youngest players ever to play in the Champions League.

Zohore signed for Fiorentina on his 18th birthday, but never made an appearance for the Italian club. Loan spells at Brøndby and IFK Göteborg between 2013 and 2014 followed, before sealing a return to his home nation with Odense Boldklub.

In 2016, Kenneth joined Cardiff on loan during the transfer window before signing permanently in the summer.

The Dane's first full season in English football yielded 12 goals in 30 appearances for the Bluebirds. The following campaign saw Kenneth play 39 games as Cardiff gained automatic promotion to the Premier League.

Last term, Zohore gained top-flight experience for the Welsh outfit and will now look to target a return with Albion.

Zohore believes his best is still to come after penning a four-year-deal with the Throstles and is excited by the challenge of scoring goals for his new club and firing Albion back to the Premier League.

Zohore said, "It's a new, big challenge for me and I'm really looking forward to playing games and scoring goals here. I want to help this club get back to the Premier League.

"I spoke to Slaven and he told me about the way he wants to play football and how he sees me fitting into the system. As a player, it's important to have a manager that believes in you and makes you feel good.

"I'm hungry to do well. Nobody has seen my best yet, but I know that it will be coming soon."

WILLOCK ON THE WING!

Jet heeled 21-year-old winger Chris Willock joined up with Slaven Bilić's squad for the 2019/20 campaign after signing a season-long loan deal from Portuguese giants Benfica.

Chris came through the Arsenal Academy and reached the first team, making his debut as a 16-year-old in a Carabao Cup tie against Nottingham Forest. But in June 2017, Willock made the switch from London to Lisbon and agreed a five-year contract with Benfica. The exciting youngster is yet to make his Benfica debut but has made over 60 appearances for Benfica B over the last two seasons.

Chris has two brothers who also play professional football. Joe plays for Arsenal and Matthew has signed for Gillingham after leaving Manchester United.

Willock, who has been capped by England at Under-16 through to Under-20 level, provides flair and creativity in forward areas and will be another strong option for Bilić to have in attack.

And now he's back in England he hopes to use experience gained on the continent and take his game to the next level.

"I'm really excited to be here and I can't wait to get started," he said.

"West Brom is a massive club and when I first heard they were interested in me it was a no-brainer for me.

" I'M REALLY EXCITED TO BE HERE AND I CAN'T WAIT TO GET STARTED. "

"I'm really pleased to be here and I'm looking forward to the future. I was really pleased that the deal went through. I'm happy to be here.

"It's definitely important that I get first team football. For the last two years, I've been in the B team, and even though that's in the second league, I think being with men every day is going to help my development and grow as a player.

"This is a huge platform to do it and I'm happy to be here to do that. I've learned a lot over the years in Portugal but I think now I'm ready to take the next step and show what I can do."

25

New head coach Slaven Bilić is, of course, a legend in Croatian football, but he isn't the first eastern European to come to The Hawthorns over the last few years.

See if you can remember these six players who have worn the stripes – and then name their countries too!

THEY CAME FROM THE EAST!

ANSWERS ON PAGE 61

26

PEREIRA WINGS IN TO THE HAWTHORNS

Winger Matheus Pereira comes to the Albion on a season-long loan from Sporting Lisbon, making him the first Brazilian-born player here since Sandro in 2016.

The 23-year-old, described on the Bundesliga website as "strong in possession, full of pace, a fine dribbler and the orchestrator of intricate interplay", spent last season in the German top division at FC Nürnberg – scoring three goals and assisting twice from 16 starts.

He moved from South America to Portugal at the age of 12, joining Trafaria as a teenager for a couple of years before linking up with Sporting.

A breakthrough into their 'B' team came by January 2014 and, just over 18 months later, he made his first-team debut during a Europa League draw against Besiktas as a 19-year-old.

No more than three weeks after that, the Belo Horizonte boy netted his maiden senior goals as they hammered Skenderbeu in Europe – and he made a total of 13 appearances in his breakthrough campaign.

The 2016/17 challenge didn't see him get as much football despite starring for their 'B' side in the second tier, and he was sent out on loan to Primeira Liga club GD Chaves for the following season.

Matheus excelled while being given regular top flight matches and helped his temporary team to a sixth-placed finish, chipping in with seven strikes and five assists from 27 showings.

The right-footed winger says his arrival at The Hawthorns is a "huge moment" in his fledgling career.

"I'm delighted to be here," he said. "It is a huge moment in my career.

"I'M DELIGHTED TO BE HERE. IT IS A HUGE MOMENT IN MY CAREER."

"I'm excited about the project and the club's ambition for the season. I want to do everything I physically can to help the club win promotion.

"I don't really like to talk much about myself. What I will say is that my team-mates, the club, the fans, the board – who have made a tremendous effort to get me here – can expect a determined, committed player.

"I will offer everything the club needs on and off the pitch. The club has my full support and I will do everything within my power to help my team-mates."

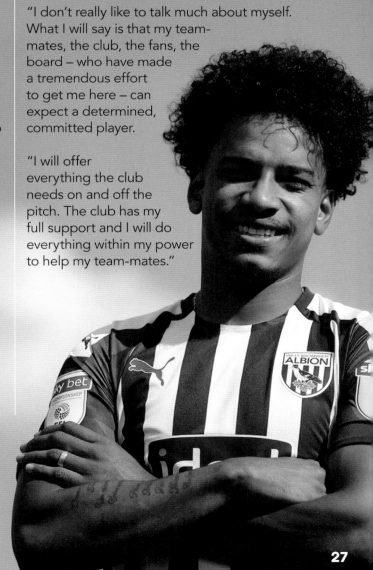

AJAYI OF THE ALBION

Versatile Nigeria international Semi Ajayi joined Albion this summer off the back of an eye-catching season at Rotherham United.

The 25-year-old, who can play as a central defender or defensive midfielder, won a series of accolades for an impressive campaign with the Millers – including Away Player of the Season and Goal of the Season.

Semi started his career at Charlton Athletic, earning his first professional contract in January 2012 after progressing through the ranks at The Valley. He spent a month on loan at then-National League team Dartford but, despite not yet playing for Charlton's first-team, he was recruited by Arsenal's Academy in September 2013.

In a couple of years at the Emirates, he featured for the senior side in friendly matches and was an unused substitute during a number of Premier League fixtures. Semi went on loan to Cardiff towards the end of the 2014/15 campaign and was then signed permanently from the Gunners that summer.

Temporary spells at AFC Wimbledon and Crewe Alexandra followed and, after a third loan away at Rotherham, United secured his services permanently in the summer of 2017.

Ajayi, who was born in London to Nigerian parents, was given his senior Super Eagles debut in September 2018 – coming on in the second half of a 3-0 Africa Cup of Nations qualifying win against Seychelles. He has since gone on to make six appearances for Nigeria.

Semi has joined on a four-year contract and has the distinction of being one of the few players able to look down on 6ft-plus Head Coach Slaven Bilić. That advantage was undoubtedly a factor in Albion's new player scoring eight goals for his former club Rotherham United last season.

"I was always a threat from set pieces and able to get on the end of things, but my conversion rate was not good enough," said Semi.

"I did a lot of work on that and last season it paid off for me. I wouldn't say I have a target because my job is to keep the ball out of our net. But I hope to weigh in with some goals again.

"I got a whisper towards the end of last season that Albion were watching me, although I didn't hear any more," he said. "I went away to play for Nigeria and thought nothing more of it but when I came back things began to start rumbling again.

"I loved the fact that they were so keen to sign me and I've come into the club and found really nice facilities and good people. The lads have been great at welcoming me.

"I know I'm not the finished article and I feel I can improve. I am playing alongside some top defenders and I think I can learn a great deal from them.

"For me it doesn't matter where you are in the league, I want to win every game and I prepare like that. But I want to play at the highest level and it's exciting to be joining a club that wants to get back there."

STRIPES FOR LIFE?

That was the slogan we used when we launched our new kit for the 2019/20 season, but now, you're in charge!

Here is your chance to design a new Albion kit, home or away, any style you like.

STRIPES OR NOT, IT'S UP TO YOU!

THE BIG QUIZ!

1
Who scored Albion's first goal of the 2018/19 season?

2
And who scored the last?

3
Which club did Sam Johnstone join Albion from?

Man. U

4
And where did Nacer Chadli go?

5
Where did Sam Field and Kyle Edwards play for England U20s in the summer of 2019?

6
Where did Chris Brunt start his playing career?

7
Who scored Albion's first ever Premier League goal?

8
When was the last time the Throstles lifted the First Division trophy?

9
Who has scored the most goals for Albion?

10
Who was the last Albion player to score at Wembley in a first team game?

11 Who was Albion's first full-time player-manager?

12 And who was the second?

13 Which club did Kyle Bartley join the Throstles from?

14 Who was Albion's top goalscorer in 2018/19?

15 Who were Albion's three degrees?

16 Which famous guitarist once featured an Albion scarf on an album cover?

17 What was the original name of the team?

18 In what year was The Hawthorns opened?

19 Who knocked us out of the League Cup in 2018/19?

20 And who was their manager?

ANSWERS ON PAGE 61

SPOT BAGGIE BIRD

Can you spot Baggie Bird supporting from the crowd?

ANSWER ON PAGE 61

FA YOUTH CUP RUN

THE KIDS ARE ALRIGHT!

Albion's youngsters enjoyed a terrific 2018/19 season with not only Rayhaan Tulloch and Morgan Rogers both making their first team debuts, but enjoying a fantastic run to the semi-finals of the FA Youth Cup to boot.

It all started with a 5-1 demolition of Lincoln City at The Hawthorns and that was followed up with a win by the same scoreline over Queens Park Rangers that took us into the last 16 of the competition.

The competition started to get much fiercer at that point and we came out of the draw with a trip to meet Arsenal's youngsters at their Boreham Wood ground, a tough task for our youngsters if they were going to progress any further.

But progress they did. The Gunners had no answer to the quality of Albion's football over the 90 minutes and, thanks to a 2-1 win, we were into the quarter-finals of the competition.

At least we had home advantage again, but we were pitted against an Everton side that had beaten us 10-0 in the Premier League Cup earlier in the season. We were able to field our full strength youth team this time though and that made the world of difference in an enthralling tie.

Fighting back from both 2-0 and 3-2 down, the young Throstles showed both quality and character to twice claw their way back into the game before finally taking the lead just 11 minutes before the end, holding onto

the 4-3 advantage to secure a first semi-final place in the FA Youth Cup since 1978.

After the game, Mike Scott, then the Under-18 Lead Professional Development Phase Coach was understandably delighted with both the performance and the result.

"It was an unbelievable comeback," he said. "I've seen quite a few comebacks from this side over the years but this one probably tops it off. To be 2-0 down and to come back and win the game in the way that we did was unbelievable really. Credit to the lads, they dug in at the end and got the result that they wanted.

"It was brilliant. It was a fantastic night for the Club, for the Academy, for the boys that have been at the Club a long, long time. It's fantastic for everybody involved."

The semi-final draw could have been kinder because we had to head north to face Manchester City at their academy stadium on the Etihad campus. It was another thrilling game that could have gone either way before Albion eventually slipped out of the competition in a 4-2 defeat. All the same, what a season to remember!

ROMAINE RETURNS

Romaine Sawyers returned to The Hawthorns this summer after leaving Brentford, some six years after he left Albion to join neighbours Walsall.

He couldn't be more pleased to be coming home to the club which launched his career through its Academy system all those years ago, joining the club as a nine-year-old.

"It's been a long time coming and feel like I have unfinished business," says Romaine.

"This is the first team that I have always wanted to play for and I'm delighted I'm now going to get that chance.

"I left the club when I was just a boy with a lot of potential. But I am coming back as a man who has matured as a player.

"It looks to me that we are assembling a st group of players and I hope to add to that. The aim is promotion – that's what we all w especially after just missing out last season.

Following his release in 2013, Birmingham born Sawyers joined Walsall, with boss at time Dean Smith citing huge potential in t versatile midfielder.

More than 150 appearances across all competitions ensued during three years in third tier at Walsall, where he netted a total 19 goals before a move to the Championsh with Brentford. There, he played 135 games and scored eight goals, as well as skippering the side.

At international level, Romaine also captains the St Kitts and Nevis side and to date has earned 26 caps.

WBA POWERCHAIR FC
POWER ON!

WFA Premiership Team of the Year, West Bromwich Albion Powerchair Football Club, had a 2018/19 season which resulted in national and international success.

Domestic joy came through clinching the Wheelchair Football Association Muscular Dystrophy UK National League title for the second year in a row.

Internationally there was plenty to smile about too as a quartet of Albion players were part of the eight-man England squad which won the European Powerchair Football Association Nations Cup 2019.

Chris Gordon, Matthew Francis, Brad Bates and Marcus Harrison were part of the team that made the trip to Finland, returning home as champions thanks to a dramatic penalty shootout victory over France in the final.

Harrison was the tournament's top goalscorer, and manager/captain Gordon said winning with England is a dream come true.

"It's not really sunk in. I've dreamt of this moment for years," said Chris, who made a crucial penalty save in the final.

"There have been a lot of sacrifices and hard work, so we're all delighted. I'm thrilled for everyone but especially the likes of Brad and Marcus who had an unbelievable tournament."

Closer to home, the second successive league title for the Albion side replicated last season's dominance, winning 20 and losing just one of their 22 games, racking up 80 goals on their way to the title.

"I'm very proud, the mentality of the players is in a different class," said Matt Bodin, WBA PFC Assistant Coach.

"They believe they deserve that medal. This isn't achieved by luck, they won it because they deserve it. The amount of goals we've scored and conceded just shows that we deserve that spot."

Matt's pride at the success was echoed by WBA PFC captain and manager, Chris Gordon.

"I am extremely proud of what we have achieved over the last two seasons," said Chris.

"With hard work and dedication, the squad have really developed and now have the honour of being the best powerchair football team in the country.

"It's our responsibility to continue to work hard to ensure that Albion's powerchair football team is widely known as the best in the country for many years to come."

There's plenty to be excited about for 2019/20 as well as they look to make it a hat-trick of titles whilst also competing in the Champions League.

Best of luck, lads!

For more information regarding Albion's powerchair programme, please email paul.hunt@albionfoundation.co.uk

THESE ARE A FEW OF MY
FAVOURITE THINGS...

JAMIE SOULE FORWARD

Football Moment: Playing for England's youth team or signing my first professional contract with the Albion.

Goal: Any of Luis Suárez's strikes for Liverpool. He always hit the ball with such skill.

Game: Liverpool winning the Champions League in 2005 because it was such an amazing comeback.

Player: Cristiano Ronaldo because he's the "Greatest of All Time"!

Stadium: Camp Nou. The atmosphere sounds breathtaking.

International Kit: Got to be England. I'd love to wear the senior shirt one day.

Boots: Adidas f50. They always fitted me perfectly.

World Cup Moment: England making the semi-final and winning 6-1 against Panama thanks to Harry Kane's hat-trick.

School Lesson: PE. I always enjoyed being out of school clothes.

Animal: I've grown up with dogs!

Colour: Blue

Chocolate: Galaxy

Drink: I think Oasis is very refreshing.

Holiday Destination: I've always wanted to visit Dubai because it looks like a beautiful place to go.

TV Show: Impractical Jokers

Car: Mercedes AMG or Lamborghini

Albion Moment: Probably the 5-5 draw against Man United, Romelu Lukaku scoring a hat-trick.

DID SAM SAVE IT?

Swansea on the attack, bearing down on the Smethwick End, with just Sam Johnstone standing between them and a goal. But did Sam save it? Which of these balls is the right one? The choice is yours!

ANSWERS ON PAGE 61

THE FINAL FURLONG!

Right-back Darnell Furlong was another of the summer of 2019 intake when he signed a four-year deal at The Hawthorns to make the move north from Queens Park Rangers.

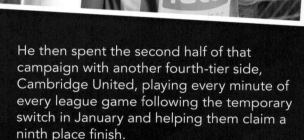

Furlong came through the ranks at QPR, signing his first professional contract with the Loftus Road side in March 2014 before making his Premier League debut just under a year later aged 19.

The Luton-born full-back, who is the son of former QPR, Birmingham City and Chelsea striker Paul Furlong, has made a total of 72 appearances for Rangers, scoring twice, as well as enjoying loan spells with Northampton Town, Cambridge United and Swindon Town.

A first loan spell came with Northampton Town during the early part of the 2015/16 season as Furlong contributed 10 appearances to the eventual League Two winners.

He then spent the second half of that campaign with another fourth-tier side, Cambridge United, playing every minute of every league game following the temporary switch in January and helping them claim a ninth place finish.

After returning to QPR that summer, Darnell was sent out to gain further first-team experience at Swindon Town in League One for the 2016/17 campaign.

He made 28 outings for the Robins in all competitions before then-QPR boss Ian Holloway recalled him to London.

He featured in 14 matches for the Hoops during the back end of that season and went on to play a total of 24 times for Rangers the following year.

The 2018/19 campaign was his most successful in terms of game time to date, with manager Steve McClaren and caretaker John Eustace employing him in 29 fixtures across all competitions.

LAUGHING GRADY

Grady Diangana believes joining Slaven Bilić at The Hawthorns is the "perfect" season-long loan move from parent club West Ham United.

The 21-year-old attacker cited a trio of motives for his move to Albion which will be music to the ears of Baggies fans.

"For me there were three factors in joining," he said. "Bilić, West Brom being a big club, and the ambition to get back in the Premier League.

"I think it's perfect. The style of play that the team has is good, the energy, the lads have welcomed me very nicely so they are a good bunch of lads, so it's good.

"I'm an attacking player. I like to create, score and assist goals. I'm a team player so I like to combine with my teammates and I always work hard and give 100 per cent.

"For me it is a very exciting time to be around in the Championship and to see how I can really stand out in such a big team.

"It gave me a lot of confidence last season to be able to play in the Premier League. Not many players get to do that so to be given the opportunity and to have done quite well in the Premier League was amazing.

"I spoke with the gaffer over the phone and he told me what his setup was like and the ambitions of the club and how he sees me in the team and how I can help the team to be better and to help push on and do well in the league.

"When he was at West Ham I was just coming through the under-23s and I started training with him a few times and travelled a few times with him and he is a very good manager.

"He is clear with what he wants from you and he will let you express yourself as long as you're always working hard.

"It brings me a lot of confidence. It shows that he believes in me and shows that he sees a lot of talent and ability in me so I want to show what I can do and hopefully win many points."

1v1 DIAGONAL ATTACK DRAG BACK

Romaine Sawyers

THE MOVE

When being challenged from the side **fake to strike the ball** but instead drag the ball back with the sole of the same foot and push off in the opposite direction using the inside or outside of the drag back foot.

COACHING POINTS

- **Exaggerate** the fake strike of the ball
- **Drag back** must be executed quickly
- Get ball out of feet to clear the incoming opponent
- To be successful the **timing of the move** is crucial

WHERE AND WHEN THE MOVE CAN BE BEST EXECUTED

STRIKER – When driving forward into the box and being challenged diagonally from the side using the drag back move will allow the player to create space to beat the defender, creating an opportunity to finish on goal.

MIDFIELDER – When dribbling forward in a midfield position and being challenged diagonally from the side, quickly performing the drag back move will allow the player to create space for a pass into the striker or wide player.

DEFENDER – When in possession of the ball outside the penalty box and facing your own goal, the drag back move would be a good option when being challenged from the side. The move would allow the player to create space and take the ball clear of the danger zone.

SKILL PRACTICE 1

- Dribble the ball slightly past the left hand cone and perform the right foot (RF) drag back move.
- Then dribble across to the other cone and perform the left foot (LF) drag back. Dribble through the middle of the two cones.
- Stop the ball and repeat the practice.

SKILL PRACTICE 2

- Start at the first cone by performing the right foot (RF) drag back.
- Proceed to the second cone and perform the left foot (LF) drag back.
- Continue up the circuit using the right foot and left foot drag back move.

IMPROVE YOUR SKILLS

1v1 FACING AN OPPONENT SIDESTEP

Kyle Edwards

THE MOVE

The player **fakes to pass the ball** with the outside of the foot but instead steps behind the ball and takes it in the opposite direction with the outside of the other foot.

COACHING POINTS

- **Use eyes and communication** to disguise the pass
- **Exaggerate** upper body movement to deceive and unbalance the opponent
- **Short step** behind the ball is all that is required

WHERE AND WHEN THE MOVE CAN BE BEST EXECUTED

STRIKER – When in or around the box and confronted with a defender face to face, using a quick side step move will allow you to create space to finish on goal.

MIDFIELDER – When attacking at an angle from a wide midfield position and being faced with an opponent, a quick side step move will allow you to create space for a penetrating pass, a cross or shot at goal.

DEFENDER – When being faced by an opponent in a defending area performing a quick side step move will allow you space to set up a forward pass into midfielder/striker or winger enabling you to set up an attack from a defensive situation.

Players **must** be aware of the various situations on the park.

SKILL PRACTICE 1

- Players work moving forward in between the 2 cones practicing the side step move.
  Step right – go left
  Step left – go right
- See how many moves you can perform and try to beat your record.

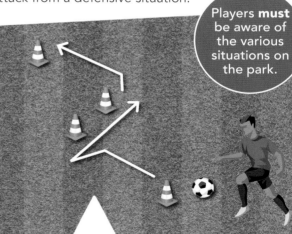

SKILL PRACTICE 2

- Dribble forward to cones and perform the left go right side step then drive forward to opposite cone.
- Repeat exercise this time performing the right go left move.
- Progression – try double side step
  Step right – left – right
  Step left – right – left

THE LONG WAY HOME!

West Bromwich Albion
Football Club

(England)

Start

Kyle Edwards is enjoying a well-earned drink after another session at Albion's training ground, but his shirt is hanging up in The Hawthorns' dressing room!

Can you help him find his way to the stadium in time for Saturday's game?

Answer on page 61

THESE ARE A FEW OF MY FAVOURITE THINGS...

PETER TAYLOR
MIDFIELDER

Goal: Wayne Rooney when he lobbed the keeper from his own half against West Ham.

Game: Sweden beating England 4-2 with Zlatan Ibrahimović's overhead kick.

Player: Sergio Busquets. He plays in my position and he's just so calm on the ball.

Stadium: Allianz Arena because of how futuristic it looks!

International Kit: Argentina, nice and simple. And it reminds me of Maradona.

Boots: The old-style Adidas Predators that Gerrard used to wear.

World Cup Moment: The goal Maradona scored against England when he dribbled past about seven players.

School Lesson: Maths – I liked the fact there was only one answer!

Animal: Dogs. I think they are friendly creatures and I love my dog.

Colour: Black

Chocolate: Galaxy Caramel

Drink: Coffee

Holiday Destination: Majorca. It's the only place abroad I've ever been.

TV Show: Match of the Day

Albion Moment: When Kieran Richardson scored to keep Albion in the Premier League.

THE RECORD BREAKERS

Do you think you know all there is to know about the Albion? You do?

Well, check your knowledge out on these two pages as we bring you the Albion record breakers!

MOST GOALS IN THE TOP FLIGHT
Ronnie Allen - 208

BIGGEST FA CUP WIN
10-1 v Chatham
2nd March 1889

OLDEST PLAYER
Dean Kiely 39 yrs 189 days
v Middlesbrough, 17th April 2010

MOST GAMES
Tony Brown - 735

YOUNGEST PLAYER
Charlie Wilson 16 yrs 73 days v Oldham Athletic, 1st October 1921

MOST GOALS
Tony Brown - 281

BIGGEST LEAGUE DEFEAT
3-10 v Stoke, 4th February 1937

BIGGEST FA CUP DEFEAT
0-5 v Leeds 18th February 1967

MOST GOALS IN A SEASON
W G Richardson - 40

MOST POINTS IN A SEASON
91 (3 points for a win) 2009/10
60 (2 points for a win) 1919/20

AUSTIN READY TO MOTOR

Goals are the key to a promotion season and Albion secured the services of a man whose SatNav is set permanently on the opposition goal when they brought in Charlie Austin from Southampton in the summer.

"It was a project that I wanted to be a part of," he said.

"I have seen that the manager is here and with the staff and the players that he has brought in and the players that are already here, it was something that I jumped at. It's a project that I want to be a part of and their goal this year is to get promotion and I want to be a part of that.

"Many years ago you would see West Brom for what it is and you see now the new manager has come in and they are trying to turn it completely around. New players have come in and with the squad they have already got here it only bodes well for the future.

"As a centre-forward you are known for your goals, that is what it is. There was only one team that scored more than Albion last year. I'm delighted to be here and as a centre-forward to score that many goals you have got to be looking to take those chances and if the team creates as many as they did last year, that bodes well for the strikers.

"I have come here to play. There's no point saying that I haven't. I have come here to start and hit the ground running, score goals and help the lads and everyone involved with the Club get promotion. That's the aim.

"It's all about me getting a run of games and I fully believe in myself, the manager has belief in me and I think when the time comes most of the lads will as well.

"I haven't set personal targets. I want to score as many goals as I can, whether it's double figures, 20, 25, 30, I don't really set them. I just want to score as many as I can and help the team and let's be honest, there is only one goal for this football club this year and that is to get promoted.

"When you move to a new club I think on the pitch stuff you can control. You can control your performances. Off the field you need to be a confident character, not too much but to integrate into the group, but they have been so welcoming to me since I came through the

CROSSWORD

We're all good friends in the Albion family, with neve[...]
except for this one!

(6 Down: SLAVAN — handwritten answer)

ANSWERS ON PAGE 61

DOWN

. The last team that we beat in an FA Cup [fi]nal (7)

. Marathon man with over 400 Albion games [t]o his name now (5, 5)

. Sam's the man in goal (9)

. The national team SuperSlav coached to [t]he 2008 and 2012 Euros (7)

. Or is Sam the man in midfield? (5)

. West Bromwich who? (6)

ACROSS

1. Legendary number 9 [...] the Brummie Road (4, 5 [...]

5. Young player of the y[...]

9. Our new head coach [...]

10. Our ground before [...]

AT THE DOUBLE FOR ALBION'S WOMEN

Albion Women had a season to remember, gaining national recognition for clinching two titles in a historic campaign.

Louis Sowe's side were crowned champions of the FA Women's National League Division One Midlands and National League Plate, the perfect way to bounce back from last campaign's relegation.

"To win the plate was a bonus for us, as the main target at the start of the season was to get promoted at the first attempt," said Louis. "For the group to have completed the double is something really special and a credit to the hard work going on at the club."

The squad had plenty of reasons to smile during 2018/19, winning 19 of their 20 matches, losing just once. Sowe's free-scoring side hit the back of the net a prolific 97 times, averaging almost five goals a game.

Their Plate victory came in impressive fashion also, with a terrific 5-1 victory over Liverpool Feds at Rugby Town Football Club.

The Baggies got off to a perfect start when skipper Hannah George curled in a magnificent free-kick from 20 yards to give Albion the advantage within five minutes. Louis Sowe's side continued to create chances with Gabbie Reid twice going close, but it was Liverpool Feds who equalised through Molly Farley, sliding the ball beneath Vannessa Kinnerley and into the back of the net.

Yet Albion regained control and deservedly moved back ahead thanks to Jess Davies, who smashed the ball home after a great spin inside the six-yard box.

PLATE COMPETITION FINAL 2019
WINNERS

Albion Women's achievements were recognised at their annual awards evening and the squad were joined by the Club's Regional Talent Centre to toast another campaign of development for the young girls.

The award winners are listed below.

Under 10s
Parents' Player: Jessica MacMurray
Players' Player: Niamh Billings
Coaches' Player: Nadene da Silva

Under 16s
Parents' Player: Mariam Mahmood
Players' Player: Thea Clearkin
Coaches' Player: Izzy Green

Under 12s
Parents' Player: Lucy Newell
Players' Player: Chiara Stokes
Coaches' Player: Grace Rogers

Development
Players' Player: Ellie Vernon
Coaches' Player: Charlie Whitehouse
Top Goalscorer: Grace Harris

Under 14s
Parents' Player: Grace Nascimento
Players' Player: Emily Fletcher
Coaches' Player: Annie Sime

First Team
Players' Player: Keeley Davies
Coaches' Player: Hannah Baines
Top Goalscorer: Natalie Murray

Congratulations to all of the players on their achievements this season.

For more information regarding Albion Women and the RTC,
please email dave.lawrence@albionfoundation.co.uk

PLAYER PROFILES

*Stats correct as of August 2019

SAM JOHNSTONE

Birthdate: 25 March 1993
Position: Goalkeeper
Height: 1.79m
Other Clubs: Manchester United, Oldham, Scunthorpe, Walsall, Yeovil, Aston Villa
Albion Games: 48
Albion Goals: 0

DARNELL FURLONG

Birthdate: 31 October 1995
Position: Right-back
Height: 1.80m
Other Clubs: QPR
Albion Games: 0
Albion Goals: 0

JONATHAN BOND

Birthdate: 19 May 1993
Position: Goalkeeper
Height: 1.96m
Other Clubs: Watford, Forest Green, Dagenham & Redbridge, Bury, Reading, Gillingham, Peterborough
Albion Games: 3
Albion Goals: 0

KIERAN GIBBS

Birthdate: 26 September 1989
Position: Left-back
Height: 1.79m
Other Clubs: Arsenal, Norwich
Albion Games: 72+2
Albion Goals: 4

SEMI AJAYI

Birthdate: 9 November 1993
Position: Centre-half
Height: 1.93m
Other Clubs: Charlton Athletic, Arsenal, Cardiff City, Rotherham United
Albion Games: 0
Albion Goals: 0

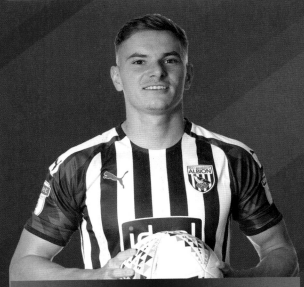

CONOR TOWNSEND

Birthdate: 4 March 1993
Position: Left-back
Height: 1.68m
Other Clubs: Hull, Grimsby, Chesterfield, Carlisle, Dundee United, Scunthorpe
Albion Games: 16+2
Albion Goals: 0

PLAYER PROFILES

*Stats correct as of August 2019

KYLE BARTLEY

Birthdate: 22 May 1991
Position: Centre-half
Height: 1.85m
Other Clubs: Arsenal, Sheffield United, Rangers, Swansea, Birmingham City, Leeds
Albion Games: 29+5
Albion Goals: 2

CHRIS BRUNT

Birthdate: 14 December 1984
Position: Winger / Left-back / Midfielder
Height: 1.87m
Other Clubs: Sheffield Wednesday
Albion Games: 348+62
Albion Goals: 47

AHMED HEGAZI

Birthdate: 25 January 1991
Position: Centre-half
Height: 1.95m
Other Clubs: Ismaily, Fiorentina, Al Ahly
Albion Games: 83+2
Albion Goals: 3

FILIP KROVINOVIC

Birthdate: 29 August 1995
Position: Midfielder
Height: 1.75m
Other Clubs: NK Zagreb, Rio Ave, Benfica
Albion Games: 0
Albion Goals: 0

JAKE LIVERMORE

Birthdate: 14 November 1989
Position: Midfielder
Height: 1.80m
Other Clubs: Tottenham Hotspur, Hull City
Albion Games: 83+10
Albion Goals: 4

REKEEM HARPER

Birthdate: 8 March 2000
Position: Midfielder
Height: 1.88m
Other Clubs: Blackburn Rovers
Albion Games: 19+6
Albion Goals: 1

PLAYER PROFILES

*Stats correct as of August 2019

ROMAINE SAWYERS

Birthdate: 2 November 1991
Position: Midfielder
Height: 1.75m
Other Clubs: Walsall, Brentford, Port Vale, Shrewsbury Town
Albion Games: 0
Albion Goals: 0

MATT PHILLIPS

Birthdate: 8 May 1998
Position: Winger
Height: 1.85m
Other Clubs: Wycombe, Blackpool, QPR
Albion Games: 79+17
Albion Goals: 13

KENNETH ZOHORE

Birthdate: 31 January 1994
Position: Striker
Height: 1.89m
Other Clubs: Copenhagen, Fiorentina, OB, KV Kortrijk, Cardiff City
Albion Games: 0
Albion Goals: 0

OLIVER BURKE

Birthdate: 7 April 1997
Position: Winger
Height: 1.88m
Other Clubs: Nottingham Forest, RB Leipzig
Albion Games: 4+17
Albion Goals: 1

KYLE EDWARDS

Birthdate: 17 February 1998
Position: Striker
Height: 1.72m
Other Clubs: None
Albion Games: 5+6
Albion Goals: 2

HAL ROBSON-KANU

Birthdate: 21 May 1989
Position: Striker
Height: 1.85m
Other Clubs: Reading
Albion Games: 33+61
Albion Goals: 9

PLAYER PROFILES

*Stats correct as of August 2019

GRADY DIANGANA

Birthdate: 19 April 1998
Position: Midfielder
Height: 1.80m
Other Clubs: West Ham United
Albion Games: 0
Albion Goals: 0

CHRIS WILLOCK

Birthdate: 31 January 1998
Position: Forward
Height: 1.78m
Other Clubs: Arsenal, Benfica
Albion Games: 0
Albion Goals: 0

CHARLIE AUSTIN

Birthdate: 5 July 1989
Position: Striker
Height: 1.88m
Other Clubs: Swindon Town, Burnley, QPR, Southampton
Albion Games: 0
Albion Goals: 0

NATHAN FERGUSON

Birthdate: 6 October 2000
Position: Defender
Height: 1.85m
Other Clubs: None
Albion Games: 0
Albion Goals: 0

MATHEUS PEREIRA

Birthdate: 5 May 1996
Position: Winger
Height: 1.75m
Other Clubs: Sporting CP, Chaves, FC Nurnberg
Albion Games: 0
Albion Goals: 0

DARA O'SHEA

Birthdate: 4 March 1999
Position: Defender
Height: 1.87m
Other Clubs: Hereford, Exeter City
Albion Games: 0
Albion Goals: 0

THESE ARE A FEW OF MY
FAVOURITE THINGS...

TAYLOR GARDNER-HICKMAN FORWARD

Football Moment: Cristiano Ronaldo's overhead kick against Juventus.

Goal: Cristiano Ronaldo's free-kick against Portsmouth.

Game: The Champions League games between Liverpool and Man City in 2018.

Player: Cristiano Ronaldo

Stadium: Manchester City's Etihad Stadium

International Kit: England's kit

Boots: Nike Mercurials

World Cup Moment: Beckham's free-kick against Greece to qualify England for the World Cup.

School Lesson: English

Animal: Dog

Colour: Blue

Chocolate: Any!

Holiday Destination: Portugal

TV Show: Any football that's on!

Film: Creed

Car: Lamborghini

Albion Moment: Jay Rodriguez's last-minute equaliser against Villa in December 2018.

QUIZ ANSWERS

Page 26: They Came From The East

1. Goran Popov, Macedonia
2. Gabriel Tamas, Romania
3. Grzegorz Krychowaik, Poland
4. Igor Balis, Slovakia
5. Robert Koren, Slovenia
6. Artim Sakiri, Macedonia

Page 30-31: The Big Quiz

1. Harvey Barnes against Bolton Wanderers
2. Craig Dawson against Aston Villa
3. Manchester United
4. Monaco
5. The Toulon Tournament
6. Sheffield Wednesday – he was a trainee at Middlesbrough but didn't play there
7. Lee Marshall v Leeds United
8. 1919/1920
9. Tony Brown
10. Kevin Donovan – 1993 play-offs
11. John Giles
12. Brian Talbot
13. Swansea City
14. Dwight Gayle
15. Cyrille Regis, Laurie Cunningham and Brendon Batson
16. Eric Clapton – Backless
17. West Bromwich Strollers
18. 1900
19. Crystal Palace
20. Roy Hodgson

Page 32-33: Spot Baggie Bird

Page 39: Did Sam Save It?

Answer: Ball B

Page 44: The Long Way Home

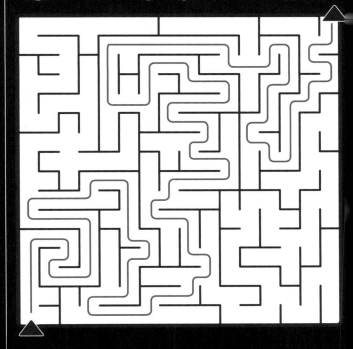

Page 49: Crossword